WHAT'S WRONG WITH MY CV?

Why can't I get a job?

© Lucy Shepherd

2012

CV is an abbreviation;
curriculum vitae

Definition of **curriculum vitae;**

*noun (plural **curricula vitae** /-lə/)*
a **brief** account of a person's education, qualifications, and previous occupations, typically sent with a job application

WHAT'S WRONG WITH MY CV?

CONTENTS

1. PROLOGUE
2. ABOUT THE AUTHOR
3. REVIEW YOUR CURRENT CV
4. WHAT SHOULD I INCLUDE?
5. 10 THINGS NOT TO PUT ON YOUR CV
6. FORMATTING YOUR CV
7. SAVING YOUR CV
8. MANAGING YOUR CV
9. 100 ACTION WORDS TO USE IN YOUR CV

PROLOGUE

WHY CAN'T I GET A JOB?

A question so many candidates are asking us.

Are you applying for vacancy after vacancy, submitting your CV to hundreds of potential employers and hearing nothing back?

Or are you managing to get through the initial application stage but failing to get through the interview?

If this sounds familiar then this series of short books will be useful for you.

There is no 100% guarantee that the advice we provide will result in immediate success, but our advice from twenty years experience of working within the Recruitment Sector will certainly help you to review your current approach, and identify ways to improve your approach to achieve success when applying for vacancies.

ABOUT THE AUTHOR

Lucy Shepherd was born in 1975 in Leamington Spa, and has worked in the Recruitment sector for 20 years.

She lives in Worcestershire, United Kingdom and now runs her own Recruitment business where she and her team recruit for a wide range of industry sectors, processing over 1000 applications per week.

Having worked for Recruitment Agencies as well as In-house within a HR function managing the Recruitment from a client perspective, Lucy has extensive experience of recruitment, and the challenges both Recruitment Agencies and Employers face when screening candidate cv's for their vacancies.

This book has been written to help candidates to review their current CV and to provide advice and guidance to help improve the content and formatting, so that it will appeal to potential employers.

WHAT'S WRONG WITH MY CV?

REVIEW YOUR CURRENT CV

WHAT'S WRONG WITH MY CV?

REVIEW YOUR CURRENT CV

Imagine sitting down to read a book.

What would you think if the book was poorly formatted? What would you think if the words were not neatly written on the page, or if the page was full of confusing words and numbers that didn't make any sense or flow as part of the story, or if there were lots of spelling mistakes?

Now imagine an employer reading your cv......

Does your cv appeal to potential employers?

We completed a study of cv's that candidate's had sent to our Recruitment Agency, and over 65% of them were poorly formatted. 55% contained spelling mistakes and 48% were more than 3 pages long.

Recruiters and employers are screening hundreds of cv's every week so if your cv lands on their desk, is it formatted in a way that will stand out above those of your competition?

Is your cv clean, concise, formatted in the same font and how many spelling, grammar or punctuation mistakes does it contain?

Now you have reviewed your own cv, please read this guide to creating a cv that will help you to get responses and results.

WHAT'S WRONG WITH MY CV?

REVIEW YOUR CURRENT CV – CHECKLIST

- ☐ Does my cv look neatly formatted?

- ☐ Is my cv only 2-3 pages long?

- ☐ Does my cv contain a short summary of my Career History as an introduction to potential employers?

- ☐ Does my cv have a maximum of 5 clear headings written in **Bold**?

- ☐ Does my cv detail my Career History in reverse order?

- ☐ Have I removed my date of birth and age from my cv?

- ☐ Is my cv spellchecked containing no spelling errors, or grammar or punctuation mistakes?

If you are answering 'No' to most of these questions then this book is definitely going to help you to review your cv and make the changes you need, to ensure your cv is presented in a way that will help you to gain the interest of employers.

WHAT'S WRONG WITH MY CV?
WHAT SHOULD I INCLUDE IN MY CV?

WHAT'S WRONG WITH MY CV?

WHAT SHOULD I INCLUDE IN MY CV?

Everyone's education and career history is different. We all have different hobbies and interests.

But what is it that employers want to know? What should you include in your cv that will attract the attention of employers and make them spend time reading your cv?

There is a famous saying "first impressions count" and that applies to your cv too!

Employers are recruiting for a job vacancy. They advertise the role in the local paper, on the job board or on their website. The advert contains information about the role and the key skills they are looking for.

When they open your cv, they want to see how your cv matches the advert – at a glance, not after reading pages and pages of irrelevant information.

- Does the job advert state that specific qualifications are required for the role?
- Does the job advert outline specific roles and responsibilities for the role?
- Does the job advert outline previous essential criteria?

This is what employers are looking for.

Easy to read, factual and concise information on your Education, Career History, Key Skills and your **Strengths.**

WHAT'S WRONG WITH MY CV?

WHAT SHOULD I INCLUDE IN MY CV – CHECKLIST

- ☐ Full name

- ☐ Short summary paragraph outlining your career history, detailing key achievements and skills relevant to the role you are applying for

- ☐ Career history in reverse date order, writing in bold the name of the Employer, Job Title and dates employed, outlining key responsibilities and skills. Make sure your career history is up to date

- ☐ Education and Memberships

- ☐ Address, telephone contact numbers and email address

WHAT'S WRONG WITH MY CV?

WHAT HEADINGS SHOULD I INCLUDE IN MY CV?

WHAT'S WRONG WITH MY CV?

WHAT HEADINGS SHOULD I INCLUDE IN MY CV?

Every book we read is sectioned off into chapters, with clear headings at the start of each chapter. This makes the book easy to read, and easy to find the section we are looking for.

Your cv should be sectioned off with clear headings so employers can read your cv, the same way they would read a book.

So what do you expect to see in a book?

Firstly a **'Title'** – the title should be your name, first name followed by last name.

Secondly you need an **'Introduction'** to your cv. A short, brief and concise outline of your career history. The introduction should be clear, concise and also relevant to the role you are applying for. The introduction is the first section employers will read, so ensure you outline your career history, and not a long list of skills or strengths or irrelevant text which will not engage the employer.

Next you need to summarise your **'Career History'** in reverse date order, so outlining your current role first, and providing a summary of your strengths and key skills for each of your previous roles.

Finally you need to outline your **Education and Memberships** providing details of the Institutions and the names of your courses with the details of the grade or level of membership.

Don't forget to insert your full name, address, contact numbers and email address at the bottom of your cv.

And finally let employers know that **References** are available on request. Don't include these in your initial cv as employers will ask for these once they've made you an offer. It saves space and unnecessary text on your cv.

WHAT'S WRONG WITH MY CV?

10 THINGS NOT TO PUT IN YOUR CV

WHAT'S WRONG WITH MY CV?

10 THINGS NOT TO PUT IN YOUR CV?

1. Your age or date of birth
2. Negative phrases
3. Your salary expectations
4. Hobbies

   (unless they are relevant to the role you are applying for)
5. Your photo
6. 'Waffle'
7. The term 'cv'
8. Too much detail
9. Spelling, grammar or punctuation mistakes
10. Personal details

    (Family information, divorce details etc)

WHAT'S WRONG WITH MY CV?

FORMATTING YOUR CV

WHAT'S WRONG WITH MY CV?

FORMATTING YOUR CV?

Now you have reviewed the content of your cv, the next thing you need to do is look at the formatting.

When you open a book, or a magazine the article or story is always neatly formatted, in the same font and aligned on the page. The text is always presented in a way that is clean, concise and in a way that will appeal to the reader.

Your cv should be formatted too.

What to consider when formatting your cv;

1. Make sure your name is the 'heading' and format in bold letters and centred at the top of the page.

2. Format headings, keywords and information specific to the role you are applying for in **'Bold'**

3. Use bullet points when detailing skills or information in a list.

4. Use the 'alignment' tool to align your cv so that it is justified to the edge of the page

5. Make sure you use the same 'font' all the way through the CV (you can increase font sizes for headings if required)

6. Use equal spacing between paragraphs

7. Don't abbreviate words or dates

7. Keep your CV concise and to the point, limiting where possible to 2 - 3 pages maximum.

8. Don't forget to spell check your cv when you've finished!

WHAT'S WRONG WITH MY CV?

SAVING YOUR CV

WHAT'S WRONG WITH MY CV?

SAVING YOUR CV?

Once your cv is typed, formatted and checked for spelling mistakes, you will need to save the cv so you can send it to potential employers.

Employers need to be able to open your cv electronically when it lands on their desk.

Recruitment Agencies will need to be able to open your cv, and edit your personal address details before sending on to their clients.

Don't save your cv in PDF format.

Make sure you save using a short, clear and professional title (e.g. Joe Bloggs curriculum vitae)

Save your document in Microsoft Word document format (.doc)

Do not add the date to your cv or to the title when you save your document. This can result in employers thinking you have more than one edition, or suggest if the date is over three months that you have been job hunting for some time!

WHAT'S WRONG WITH MY CV?

MANAGING YOUR CV

WHAT'S WRONG WITH MY CV?

MANAGING YOUR CV

In the next e-book we provide guidance and support in applying for vacancies, deciding which roles to apply for and managing your cv through the application process.

One of the biggest mistakes candidates make is 'saturating' the marketplace with their cv.

Submitting cv's to too many Recruitment Agencies and to employers directly can result in potential employers receiving your cv more than once.

This can make you look 'desperate' and also demonstrates poor management of your cv through the application process.

Make sure you only apply for roles once (directly or indirectly) and ensure you manage who has your cv, and who it is being submitted to at all times.

Manage your cv - do you know where it is right now?

WHAT'S WRONG WITH MY CV?

100 ACTION WORDS TO USE IN YOUR CV

WHAT'S WRONG WITH MY CV?

100 ACTION WORDS TO USE IN YOUR CV

Accelerated	Established	Planned	Stressed
Accomplished	Ended	Pioneered	Strengthened
Achieved	Ensured	Presented	Stretched
Activated	Exceeded	Processed	Succeeded
Approved	Extended	Programmed	Summarised
Attained	Finalised	Positive	Superseded
Budgeted	Finished	Profit	Supervised
Built	Forecast	Promoted	Terminated
Calculated	Foresaw	Questioned	TraIned
Conceived	Generated	Rectified	Traded
Conducted	Headed	Recognised	Transformed
Completed	Increased	Redesigned	Translated
Consolidated	Implemented	Reduced	Tripled
Contribution	Improved	Reorganised	Trimmed
Controlled	Introduced	Rescued	Turned
Core	Invented	Researched	Uncovered
Created	Launched	Revised	Unified
Delegated	Led	Revived	Utilised
Delivered	Maintained	Saved	Verified
Demonstrated	Motivated	Scheduled	Waged
Designed	Negotiated	Set up	Won
Diagnosed	Ordered	Sold	Worked
Directed	Operated	Solved	Wrote
Doubled	Perceived	Sorted	
Eliminated	Performed	Started	
Empowered	Persuaded	Streamlined	

www.ingramcontent.com/pod-product-compliance
Lightning Source LLC
Chambersburg PA
CBHW061523180526
45171CB00001B/312